The Art of Appreciation

Leonard Chatman Jr.

Chat4You Publishing
author@leonardchatmanjr.org

© Copyright – 2020

All Rights Reserved. No part of this book may be reproduced, stored in a retrieval system, or transmitted by any means without the written permission of the author.

Cover Design: Zjae Productions

ISBN-13: 978-0-578-23064-1

Printed in the United States of America

Acknowledgements

First and foremost, I want to give all honor and glory to my Lord and Savior Jesus Christ. Without his presence, protection and love toward my family, I would not have been able to complete this book.

To my mommy, Cheryl Chatman: You are one of the most loving, spirited and supportive individuals in my corner. I'm so appreciative of everything you have done for my brother and me, and we are truly indebted to you. The sacrifices you continually make will never go unnoticed, and I thank you for everything from the bottom of my heart.

To my dad, Dr. Leonard Chatman Sr: You taught me how to be a man, and you continually provide me daily wisdom and insight. I'm thankful for your presence and proud to be your son. Thank you for your support, our moments of laughter and your example of what a great man should look like.

To my wife, Monique Chatman: Baby, you continually amaze me each day we are together. Your support you continually demonstrate is what has allowed me to complete this book. I'm so thankful to have you in my corner and even more proud to call you my wife.

To my children: While you have yet to enter into this amazing world, everything I do is for YOU. I love you, and I pray this book will provide the example of how to live your life.

To my amazing grandparents, Richard & Dorothy Coffey, June & Sarah Lundy, Jackie Chatman and the late Reginald Chatman: I feel your presence and love every day. Thank you for your words of wisdom, and your love is something that pushes me daily.

To my great-grandparents, the late Herbert & Letha Nicholson: This book is dedicated to the two of you. When I was a kid, I watched you value the lives of others before your own, and that gave me the first glimpse of what appreciation looks like. The sacrifices each of you made for our family are the glue that has kept us together. Thank you for shining down from heaven with your love. I love you and miss you tremendously.

Table Of Contents

Acknowledgments		iii
Introduction		ix
Chapter 1	The Power of Gratitude	1
Chapter 2	Thanksgiving Year-Round	11
Chapter 3	Appreciation Over Evaluation	23
Chapter 4	Appreciation in the Workplace	33
Chapter 5	Sow Your Seed	45
Chapter 6	Row The Boat	55
Chapter 7	Lengthen Your Runway	65

Introduction

Appreciation has become a forgotten and neglected concept in the world we live in, but if an individual, family, business or organization is open to the ideology, it can be the greatest unwrapped gift of the generation. If we all became fully transparent and allowed ourselves to enter a space of vulnerability, I'm confident the overwhelming consensus would be that everyone wants to be appreciated and valued in some capacity. One of the main reasons I said, "If we became fully transparent and allowed ourselves to enter a space of vulnerability," is due to the person that says…

- I don't need the accolades.
- Feeling appreciated is not my love language.
- I don't need any "pats on the back."
- Words of affirmation are not a need of mine.

The truth of the matter is EVERYONE has either a vocal desire or unsaid need to feel valued or appreciated on some level.

I've often wondered why it is so challenging for some to express appreciation for who people are and the value they bring to the table. I may not have all the answers, but one thing that has become quite obvious is the energy of envy and jealousy. I remember growing up in Jacksonville, Florida, on the west side of town, hearing my mom and great-grandmother tell my brother and me to get in the house before the streetlights came on. Of course, that was for our safety, but it was also a time for them to give us very important life lessons that would essentially be the cornerstone guiding tools of our lives moving forward. One of the major lessons I recall vividly was, "Always try to see the other person's viewpoint. Possibly one of my favorites was, "Make sure you always smile, because it comes over in your voice." Those things are still relevant to my very existence, but quite honestly the core of those enriching lessons is appreciation for others. Let me be clear before we engage any further that, for whatever reason, there are going to be some individuals whose language of communication will never be appreciation, whether it's on the giving or receiving side. I have my theories on why people reject appreciation from others. One of my personal theories is the root of negativity. Have you ever encountered someone, and you admired their outfit or something they possessed? Maybe it was a purse or a nice pair of earrings. For the fellas, maybe it was their sports coat or briefcase. Whatever was admired, you took effort in sharing your kind thought, but the person was so negative that all you got was crickets, when the proper response should have been, "Thank you" or better yet, after your compliment someone laughed.

I can almost guarantee that someone reading this knows exactly what I'm talking about when it comes to the parallel between appreciation and negativity. Some people have taken residence in complaining for so long that they don't know how to receive compliments and they have grown so accustomed to criticism that compliments appear mystifying.

In this book, The Art of Appreciation, the greatest unwrapped gift is that we will explore various ways to appreciate others for not only what they do, but more importantly for who they are. The root of building the most organic sustainable relationships is the demonstration of sincere appreciation. I believe that the sole reason we were put on this earth was to build authentic relationships. Every moment of our day is dealing with people. From the time we wake up to us lying down for the evening is spent interacting with people.

No matter how you slice the concept, relationships are very much a part of our existence. From a spiritual perspective, business understanding or personal viewpoint relationships are at the heartbeat of everything that we do.

My philosophy is not complicated, but rather quite simple. Knowing what I just shared, wouldn't it make sense to know how to manage people? One of the ways to do so is expressing sincere appreciation for the overall person. Of course, the pessimist will not want to become a thought partner in this concept and will give rebuttal with the notion that some people don't need appreciation (which is true), but I can guarantee that everybody (and I mean everybody) wants to be valued. Whether professional relationships, personal relationships or interpersonal interactions, everybody wants to be valued. Let me take it a step further than that, walk across the ledge and say not only does everybody wants to be valued, but EVERYBODY IS VALUABLE. This book is not just about giving a pat on the back or the warmth and fuzziness associated with appreciation, but the true essence of humanizing individuals because we all have some magnitude of worth. My goal while you read and engage with me on this journey is to tap into an inner space that travels down the road of valuing everyone regardless of where they may come from, in spite of their prestige or lack thereof, or what they can or cannot do for you. Apart from all of that, let's locate some area to exude appreciation toward one another.

Chapter 1

"The Power of Gratitude"

Before we truly start with anything, and for you to get the most of the book as a reader, the clearest definition for gratitude must be given. Actually, it's already been given in the introduction, "appreciation." I would be remiss in my responsibility as an author and speaker if I didn't give you more substance than that. Gratitude is the effort taken to acknowledge someone or something. The key words are "effort" and "acknowledgment." Those two words possess a chief characteristic that many in this world struggle with, and that is selflessness. The removal of oneself to impact another is the greatest model of expressing gratitude and value. In honest transparency, showing gratitude does take effort, but it's a rewarding feeling rather than an exhausting ordeal. The power of gratitude is not just rewarding for oneself, but for everyone involved. Think of it from this perspective: We were put on this earth to develop, galvanize and cultivate relationships. So shouldn't we in return understand the power of placing full appreciation on people we are in relationship with? I almost know what you're thinking right now: "I'm not in a relationship with everyone." My rebuttal is, "YES YOU ARE!" The first thing we must do is rid ourselves of preconceived notions about relationships.

The Art of Appreciation

Relationships do not have to be your typical boyfriend, girlfriend or "Can I date you?" type of scenario. A relationship can look like you and the janitor at the neighborhood grocery store speaking to each other every morning. What you just did was valued who the person is versus what the person does. I strongly believe that one of the chief characteristics regarding gratitude is appreciating who the person is. Proper value placed on people, returns an empowered person. What does that mean? When people feel valued they tend to feel empowered to return the same value towards someone else. Sitting at the bedside of my great-grandmother just before she transitioned to her eternal resting place, she would tell me as a young man that "Gratitude goes a long way." Those melodious words could not be truer to this day. People have left companies because they were not valued, and people have changed church affiliations because they were not valued.

As you read this book open your hearts and minds to the idea that people matter first as human beings over what they can or cannot do for you. I wrote this book with the person in mind first because, throughout my life I've witnessed on many occasions and have spoken to thousands of people who felt that their voice was either not heard or simply not valued. I know we live in a world full or individuals who tend to think of self first, and I totally understand that concept and ideology. What if we took the alternative approach and investigated what our neighbor needed or how we could

The Art of Appreciation

serve them today? Our world would be stronger. Truthfully, there is power in gratitude. Gratitude makes a person feel desired. Gratitude makes a person feel wanted, and gratitude will make a person work 10 times harder. Gratitude has the power to change attitudes for the better. Gratitude will move a disgruntled employee to an overachiever. Gratitude will change the entire energy of a tense meeting. Gratitude will turn a frown into a smile. Look how amazing the power of gratitude could be if only we deployed it in the spaces and organizations that we occupy. Let me be completely honest in that showing or expressing gratitude does not have to be an exaggerated, cheesy, over-the-top escapade. It can be a simple, sincere, kind and thoughtful gesture. Earlier I mentioned relationships, and here's the thing about relationships that we tend to forget. Relationships require effort. It's not necessarily a large effort, but the biggest factor is that people want to know that you are trying. Gratitude mirrors the same concept as relationships, with the simple concept that if you just give a little effort and demonstrate the capacity to appreciate someone for who they are and what they may bring to the table, then you have won a friend.

We've identified how the power of gratitude can change the whole trajectory of someone's behavior, someone's mindset or the whole energy of a meeting. Most times your gratitude can change the energy of the interactions you may have with an individual. Now let's move from identification to activation. In the next phase of this chapter, I provide some "How-to tips" to move your gratitude from identification to activation.

- Take a moment out of your day and send an email to someone who has played an instrumental role in your professional life. Share with them how impactful they are or have been toward your professional development.
- Intentionally, call a loved one just to say hello, say I love you or, better yet, take them out to lunch.
- Surprise your spouse with a special Hallmark card or personalized note with their favorite candy.

I implore you not to think of these as a transactional items, but rather as actionable items. If you go into these pursuits with the wrong thinking, your intentions will not come over as pure. Let me share an example. Doing something out of spite demonstrates your inability to do it from the heart, and typically that is accompanied by an aroma. That aroma I am mentioning can be sniffed a mile away most of the time. Disingenuous actions never come off very well because they are never sincere, so I encourage you to do a heart check before you take any action.

I have learned that the power of gratitude should prevail, but often is neglected, within families. The reason gratitude is often neglected in families is because of just that, "family." For some, they

The Art of Appreciation

have taken on this mantra that because we are family that conveys a sense of entitlement, and that is far from being accurate. The truth is gratitude extends to everyone regardless of the relational dynamic. There was a young man who attended his family church practically his entire life. After going off to seminary to hone his craft of preaching, he began working with his grandfather around the church doing whatever he could put his hands on to do. From ministry organization to evangelistic outreach, preaching on Sundays and even custodial efforts, this young man wanted to assist in any capacity. For a series of months and possibly years this young man was disrespected, devalued and disregarded by his grandfather who was the Senior Pastor, the audio/media personnel and even the minister of music. The members of the church loved this young man, but over time the leadership did not fully respect this young man. Ultimately, this young man left the family church for many reasons, but the root of it was that he was not valued, respected or appreciated. Why? There are several variables to it, but in the end the expectation was that this young man was always going to be around because he was "family." Showing gratitude and understanding the power of it is not hard; we make it hard.

Chapter 2

Thanksgiving Year-round

Every year on the fourth Thursday of November, families gather together around the dinner table and enjoy a delicious feast. For some, on this fourth Thursday of November, they make a conscious effort to give back to the community by serving meals to the homeless. In many families men sit around the television and watch the NFL football games throughout the day. This day is commonly known as Thanksgiving. On this day many find time to reflect on all the things they have to be thankful for, whether it be materialistic, tangible or even the fact that there is still opportunity to breathe.

What a wonderful day Thanksgiving has become—getting together with loved ones, sharing laughs, and catching up with those who you haven't seen in while. For many years I have had a thought in question form: What if we created a culture of Thanksgiving year-round? What if we could extend the climate of Thanksgiving Day to EVERY DAY? What if the aroma (not the smell of food) of Thanksgiving Day lasted much longer than the 24 hours that we traditionally celebrate?

Let's be honest—the fundamental, grassroots essence of Thanksgiving is "APPRECIATION." Of course everyone appreciates the wonderful meal prepared (I do), but what about appreciating the fact that there is yet another opportunity to be in the presence of loved ones, or better yet be in the presence of people in general regardless of who is the most successful in the family, or who's driving what car this year? Just organic appreciation. That's the culture we should hunger for in life is—appreciating others for "WHO" they are and not "WHAT" they are, which are two distinctive things.

Let's explore the differences between the **WHO and the WHAT**.

Who are you? **You're fearfully and wonderfully made.**

Who are you? **You're somebody.**

Who are you? **You're valuable.**

Who are you? **You're gifted and talented.**

The WHO travels the road of your DNA and what you bring to the table, just like the Thanksgiving Day dinner. While some may bring sweet potato pie, another may bring apple cobbler, but either dessert is still something of value, for it can provide nourishment and sweet satisfaction. Granted, those desserts come with different ingredients, different styles and of course a different flavor, but in the end the result is nourishment. That's how I look at the bigger picture of life and the sense of valuing and appreciating people, just like those two incredibly different desserts. People are different; their "flavor" or how they may do certain things may be quite different from yours, but in the end, the ultimate result should be you developing a work ethic in locating an opportunity to appreciate the individual as a whole. As I mentioned, people are different, and that is the true beauty of living, because if we all looked alike, spoke the same language, had the same voices and wore the same clothes, how boring would that be? Actually, I'll go beyond "boring" and say that nothing would get accomplished because we would have the same talent and same gifts, producing the same results. So, I appreciate and find value in those with gifts unlike mine. I appreciate those who excel tremendously where I'm weak because, as the old proverb states, "We get more done together than alone." The WHO can sometimes be tough for some because we all get in such a routine, and many choose to remain in their lanes. But there is something special about the treasure of WHO because often you'll find encouragement, joy, peace, happiness, perspective, understanding and a beautiful smile once you dive into someone's WHO. Most times, discovering someone's WHO requires a certain type of heartbeat. The rhythm of this heartbeat should flow with compassion and understanding. The reason for that is because what you find on the other side may not be what you expect. Always remember that your rhythm (Compassion and Understanding) should outweigh your routine. (Focus on self).

Think of it from this perspective: What if you took the time out of your day to have lunch with a homeless individual? You begin talking to them and they begin sharing about their life story. Little did you know this same individual that has been living on the streets for the last three years is actually a

The Art of Appreciation

college graduate, a veteran of the U.S. Armed Forces, and once earned a six-figure salary. We can speculate and make distasteful assumptions about what led up to this individual's collapse and loss of grip on life, but the moral to the story is behind what you see is someone of value, and that is why we must appreciate people because there is always something greater behind what we see on the exterior. There is always something special beyond what we see externally from people. If you develop the work ethic to see the good in people first versus imagining the worst first, on the other side can be the love, joy, peace and happiness that you've been hungering for. I mentioned in my last book that the encouragement that you may need could possibly come from someone you least expect. Thus, the importance of value and appreciation is paramount.

Now that we've taken care of the WHO, let's tackle the WHAT. I remember growing up watching my mom and dad facilitate workshops across the country, and one of the things they would mention is the "WIIFM" concept. "What's In It For Me?" Mom and Dad would share with their audiences that this thought process is toxic to relationship building and more importantly appreciating others. The WHAT concept typically comes with an expiration date because they, whoever "they" are, can decide at any given moment to terminate "What" they are doing for you. So, what did you appreciate more? What they did for you or them as a person? The value you place on the "what" of an individual typically does not

The Art of Appreciation

have a happy ending because once the resources run out, often the relationship ends because of where the focus was placed.

One of the most critical components to relationship building is appreciating who the person is and not what they can do for you. Think of it from this perspective and analogy. You're invited to a networking event and there are hundreds of professionals interacting with each other. In this particular space are people from different walks of life, various professions from executives to your neighborhood repair man, and then you walk in. You find yourself overwhelmed at where to begin or even what to do, but you know your goal is to make connections. You begin to interact with different individuals, and instead of learning about what others' occupations are, you overpower the conversations with your business with the intent of seeing how they can help scale your company or endeavors. What a major turnoff that is because the whole idea of networking summits is to identify where can I build the strongest relationship and not whom can I connect with so they can help me. It's the same concept with painting a canvas of appreciation, for we are built to value people first and the benefits are secondary to everything else.

Here's another aspect of the "what" scenario we may want to consider. When purchasing a car, as soon as it is driven off the lot, the value depreciates. The million-dollar question is why does the car lose its value upon exiting the dealership's parking lot? Here's your answer. The car depreciates immediately because it is being used. Over a considerable amount of time the car will lose even more value due to the usage. The same ideology goes for people. People are generally inclined to be helpful, but they don't want to feel used because their value depreciates. Let's admit it—being used is not a warm and fuzzy feeling, but when you can help or assist someone reach their highest potential or their goals, that's when the rewarding feeling begins to take place. My hope is that you adopt the concept of sharing the spirit of Thanksgiving Day, EVERY DAY.

Chapter 3

Appreciation over Evaluation

Prior to working as an entrepreneur, I enjoyed (sometimes) a great career in the healthcare arena serving in various capacities that allowed me the opportunity to work and manage many individuals. As a manager, I took full responsibility for the growth of my team as a whole as well as each individual. That being said, a great majority of my responsibility as the boss and leader was to provide feedback through evaluative assessments. From quarterly feedback meetings and semi-annual evaluations to the infamous annual assessment, I ensured that our department was in compliance. I recall vividly during my tenure in the United States Navy having evaluations completed periodically. It was a very tense and pressure-filled time because the culture and assumptions were that if you don't score well on your "eval," it could affect your ability to be promoted downstream. The struggle I've always had with "evals" or whatever term used to determine your performance has been that it typically comes off as a very subjective process. What if the person evaluating you has a bias against you? What if the person evaluating doesn't care for you, and you haven't done a single thing to deserve that "dislike"? All of those factors have been on replay in my mind throughout my career. Could I possibly be the only individual that has even thought of that perspective?

The Art of Appreciation

Here's how we combat that. Of course the inevitable is to identify areas of opportunity for the professional to be evaluated based on their performance and their contribution towards the team and departmental goals, but one of the many things I came to understand through this process is placing value on the person first and what they brought to the team. I adopted the role of appreciator first and then evaluator. Of course, I had to draw a line in the sand when necessary, but I did not allow certain factors to cloud the person's overall performance. I've realized over time that we all have had some bad days and there will be pockets where we may not score a touchdown in our work week, but I've always felt that it's totally unreasonable to think that someone is going to be on their

"A game" for all 365 days a year, 7 days a week, so I learned to extend grace and cut people some slack. It doesn't negate that I expected and demanded much from my staff. Quite honestly, I expected each of them to do their jobs at a very high level and when we did that, reaping the rewards felt so much better. Think about it—Michael Jordan, as great as he was during his NBA playing career (possibly so great he could still play right now), did not make every shot, but he kept taking the shot. Wayne Gretzky, one of the greatest NHL players of all time, did not score on every possession, but he kept skating anyway. Tiger Woods, who happens to be me my favorite golfer does not (and let me repeat does not) get eagles and birdies on every hole, which kind frustrates me, but

The Art of Appreciation

sometimes he has to settle for par or even worse a bogey.

Why is that so critical to our understanding and this chapter? In modern society, we've become so critical, judgmental, harsh and hard (and the list goes on) when it comes to people. The immediate misconception could be that I, as the author, desire only the warm fuzzies without anything of the contrary. That is far from the reality when, in fact, I welcome wholeheartedly constructive feedback, but I draw the line of delineation when evaluation of others is your only identifier. What I encourage others to do is sincerely develop a work ethic in learning people and who they are to their core. You can't bake a pie without the crust. The crust is the core and you add everything else after that. Not only that, I'm pretty certain that you have never witnessed anyone bake a pie in their living room. Why is that? Because the tools necessary for any recipe to work are located in the kitchen, such as the oven, pots, bowls and whatever else required for the success of a great tasting pie. That's exactly how life works—if you want to develop others and witness improvement and true change, then you must go in the "kitchen" and put in some work because it will not come to you on a silver platter.

Taking the highway of appreciation first allows for any individual to acknowledge the person first without having anything added. This road makes people feel welcomed, accepted, affirmed, received and most importantly valued. Let's all be honest—EVERYONE wants to feel valued,

The Art of Appreciation

and that's the true indicator for appreciation.

Let me share with you a story about NASA's mission control in Houston. During the pre-planning and pre-launch activities of Apollo 13 (1970), there was said to have been hundreds upon hundreds of meetings with personnel staff from the lowest to highest on the hierarchy. The idea of having so many meetings was of course due to the gravity of the mission. Everyone needed to understand the seriousness of the situation and to ensure everyone was on the same page. Another fundamental reason for having so many meetings was to create a culture around the entire mission control center, based on the shared assumption that everyone was needed, regardless of position, to pull off such a historic mission.

Everyone was bought in so much about the mission that the NASA flight director stepped outside one day to get some fresh air and overheard one of the janitors speaking to who he thought was someone else, but in reality, it was himself. The janitor was filled with so much joy that the flight director asked him, "What are you so excited about?" The janitor's response was, "I'm on the team to get man to the moon!" The janitor's response surprised and stunned the director because he didn't realize how strong the culture was until he ran into this janitor.

How cool is that? That's exactly how life should play out. The janitor was not a decision-maker, but he felt just as part of the mission as the man who was in charge. Regardless of where you come from, your socioeconomic landscape, your title or lack thereof, everyone should be valued and appreciated without the initial evaluation perspective. If this ideology takes fire, like a disease being coined an epidemic, that is when we will begin to see true change. It's also a biblical principal that is easily transferred into the marketplace. The scripture states in Matthew 7:1, "Judge not, that you will not be judged also. For the same judgment the individual has judged, it shall be judged against you the same." The concept of that passage is sharing that no matter who we are, there is absolutely no room to judge anyone because we all have stumbled, we all have fallen short and we all have idiosyncrasies that may plague us. But we are all one, and we are all humans.

Chapter 4

Appreciation in the Workplace

The old saying goes, "People leave companies, and they also leave managers because of not feeling valued in their role." That is absolutely correct! For starters, I am a witness to that quote's truth because I have lived it through and through. During my corporate career, I worked for a company (name shall remain anonymous), and my boss at the time (name shall also remain anonymous) unquestionably gave me the absolute hardest time known to mankind. I couldn't understand for the life of me why they would create a culture of maliciousness until it dawned on me soon after I left. Could it have been that they didn't show me appreciation because they didn't value themselves? The climate at the time was quite dogmatic towards the employees and it made coming to work very difficult. The retention rates in the corporate sector will continue to plummet if those in leadership positions choose not to value those who report to them. Businesses, companies, nonprofits and practically anyone who has employees must understand the critical importance of appreciating those who work for them and not run them off. In this chapter, I will discuss tools and strategies to keep employees happy and not give them a hunger to search for outside employment. I will also share some insight on the things that have been shared with me over the years, both from happy employees that kept

The Art of Appreciation

them stationary and from frustrated employees that decided to resign for various reasons. My hope is that the feedback that I'm sharing in this chapter and the strategies that I will be providing will be utilized so that businesses can thrive, careers are strengthened and lives are changed for the better.

The first of many tools that we will pull out of our box for this chapter is called the "Deposit Wrench." If you know anything about a wrench, its principle function is to apply enough pressure to an object for it to TURN. I'm sure the overwhelming consensus as it pertains to the workplace is that pressure is applied on a daily basis whether it's knowingly or unknowingly. What if we transformed some of that pressure into deposits of appreciation, deposits of gratitude and deposits of value? If we truly want employees to turn the corner of performing at their highest potential and maximizing their talent trajectory, then we must pull out our deposit wrenches from the toolboxes. It's undeniable that wrenches are designed to apply the necessary pressure to achieve its desired goal of tightening a bolt or loosening a nut, but just imagine if we deposited weekly, monthly, or quarterly deposits of gratitude to those employees who deserve acknowledgement. I have heard many accounts that those in leadership capacities are eager and enthusiastic about diagnosing or dissecting deficiencies, but hesitant to celebrate. The formula is backwards, as we should be excited to celebrate. Being excited to celebrate creates a culture that we care about you, and being enthusiastic to appreciate demonstrates value of wanting people to become victorious. That is what will keep top talent in the workplace. The largest message that I want to convey is summed up in one word—intentionality. Executives, HR professionals and leaders must be intentional about recognizing those who have done a good job. Intentionality + appreciation = strong culture.

The second tool we will pull out is the "Creativity Drill." This tool is possibly one of my favorites because it's actually one of the corporate terms that was "drilled" (no pun intended) into my brain during my career. As it pertains to value creation and appreciation creation, there must be creativity. There were so many moments during my career in which processes, newly designed systems and in some cases policies and procedures were heavily drilled down from the top to the bottom. Utilizing these strategies will build positive morale.

I completely understand budget constraints, but there are ways to become creative with a very low-cost approach. Certificates are great, but plaques are greater. Luncheons are awesome, but a half-day off is even more rewarding. The ability to become creative in your approach to valuing or appreciating immediately conveys to the recipient intentional thoughtfulness.

Intentional thoughtfulness is the breakthrough sometimes needed to bridge the gap between retention and recruitment. Retention is the ability to sustain and maintain a healthy culture for your employees to grow, but recruitment can sometimes be the need to fill the room because talent has left. As leaders we must always be mindful how to differentiate between the two.

The ultimate objective and end goal is to display demonstrative appreciation through intentional thoughtfulness. The late President Teddy Roosevelt famously coined the phrase, "People don't care how much you know, until they know how much you care." One of the greatest ways to demonstrate you care is becoming creative in your appreciation.

The third and final tool that we will pull from our workplace appreciation toolbox is called the "Tool Holder." This is one of the most important items that we will discuss because having this visible will strengthen and organically change your workplace culture for the better. What is a tool holder? A tool holder is an object that allows you to visibly hang your tool successfully with easy access. The importance of this tool is summed up in one word—access.

When something is accessible, it typically is in plain view for others to see and within reach for everyone to use. Culture is built from the top down and not the contrary. A wise proverb said, "A fish rots from the head down," meaning that everything comes from the top. If the employees see that the leaders are valuing others and being demonstrative in their appreciation towards others, it will flow down even to the janitor. Here's the caveat.

The Art of Appreciation

If employees do not have an understanding of this concept, that's where the "Tool Holder" comes into effect because leaders will see the importance and create systems, establish resources and organize action plans to ensure that everyone is immersed in the culture of valuing each other regardless of title or position. One of my clients that has hired me to speak to their employees is Starbucks. While I have spoken at many places, sometimes in front of thousands, Starbucks is at the top of my list of positive cultures through appreciation. This well-known and established company doesn't recognize its workers as "employees" but as "partners." How cool is that! How true is that? Starbucks realized the valuable roles that people play in ensuring that businesses are successful by saying, "We are partners, and we value you so much that regardless of title or position we're in this together." Starbucks does an enormous number of things to express appreciation consistently versus bottling it up in one annual luncheon. I encourage leaders to create a culture of taking the time out to say, "Thank you," and that will go a long way. When I worked for Aetna Better Health of Kentucky, the CEO at the time, Mr. Terence Byrd, intentionally took the time out to step away from his desk and walk the floors for at least 15 minutes periodically throughout the week just to say hello and "Thank you" to everyone working. As busy as he was, that said so much about his character, integrity and leadership philosophy. Those are moments that I will never forget, and I hope after this chapter each of you commit to strengthening your respective workplaces and those who walk through the doors.

Chapter 5

Sow Your Seed

No matter who you are, or how strong emotionally you may be, whenever someone gives you an encouraging word, it surely feels good and goes a long way. I believe it's inside every living being to enjoy or feed from positive, affirming words. Growing up, our neighbors had a dog, and for the most part it was a good dog until some of the neighborhood kids would bark and antagonize it. One day I believe this dog grew weary of basically being bullied, and it unleashed a flurry of bites to those teenagers. Now it may seem like a stretch of a story, although it's true, just imagine if those same kids would have given the dog a nice pet or been a little bit warmer, the outcome might have been different. That's how life can be as it pertains to our interactions with people—if we would be just a little bit more kind or nice, maybe individuals wouldn't be so quick to "bark" or "bite" back. The title of this chapter is centered around planting and the return on what has been sown.

Everything about our very existence is about planting and growing. All the way down to eating healthy food is based on plant-based or grown products versus packaged products. The healthiest route to eating is eating those things that come from seeds. Vegetables are healthy and come from some form of a seed. My perspective on life is that the healthiest individuals find themselves either sowing something positively or planting something positively. Planting and gardening are all-time favorite activities passed down from century to century. Whether it was planting grass seeds, fruit and vegetables in the garden, or planting words of encouragement, they all work hand in hand with the same concept.

That concept I speak of is that what you plant, you will see return. My focus for the duration of this chapter will be on the "What" you are planting versus the "When" with regards to the return. The only control you have in this process is what you are planting. You have zero control over when you will receive a return on the investment, but I can almost guarantee that one day you will receive it.

Would you believe me if I shared that one day in my backyard, I planted a watermelon seed, and then time passed, with several days of rain and multiple trips outside in the sun to water what began to grow over a period of time. Eventually we had a nice green watermelon. It was absolutely the coolest thing to witness something grow from seed to product. That's how life works. The proverb says, "What you give will be what you get." Although it's a simple concept, sometimes we miss the mark, but those reading this book and particularly this chapter can commit themselves to not missing this mark. If we are to change our neighborhoods for the better, if we are going to strengthen families positively, then we must be mindful of what we are sowing. According to

The Art of Appreciation

Webster's Dictionary, the word "sow" means "to be thickly covered with and caused to appear or spread." Let me dispel a notion for those that attend churches that sowing has to be a monetary gesture. Sowing most times is about what you say and what you are doing versus what you have to give.

Let's chat about the first principle of sowing, and that is "what we say." Words have power, and words take on life once they are spoken. Words can either birth partnerships or they can poison relationships. When I speak, my words should be affirming, positive, encouraging, uplifting and enhancing. Words are so crucial because they can either derail someone's dreams or detour someone from going down the wrong path. We must affirm people even when they don't fully match the affirmation you are giving. For example, I was the keynote speaker at a teacher symposium, and one of the audience members approached me after my speech and expressed how down and tired she was until she sat there and listened to what I was sharing. She left there energized, motivated, uplifted and empowered. Affirming words can sustain and provide you with the fuel needed for your life's car to keep moving.

Now that we understand how important it is to know what we say can determine the outcome of the things we experience, we can now transition to possibly the most challenging part, which is "what are we doing." I believe the "what are we doing" component is challenging for

The Art of Appreciation

some because our society and culture have come to emphasize:

1) Stay in your lane
2) Do your own thing
3) Mind your own business

Those are true statements within some contexts, but not for this chapter or book. One of my favorite words in the dictionary is comeUNITY. Yes ma'am and yes sir, I intentionally spelled it wrong from the original "community." If we are to change the narrative of valuing people and painting the art of appreciation across the world, we must come together as one in true unity. I love the word because that's the essence of everything we do in life, bridging things and people together. If you're building a house, the architect is bringing the foundation and structure together. If you're building a table, the carpenter is bringing the top and legs together to complete the full product. We must move past the concept that this is a white community, or black community or Asian community, but this is our community.

The "what we are doing" aspect is also birthed from a time when I needed my neighbors the most, and it didn't matter what I had to offer. The only thing they asked was, "What do you need?" I recall vividly that I had run out of gas possibly five miles from my home. Of course, in hindsight, I should have stopped at the gas station, but after a long day at work I was just ready to get home. Once the car stopped and I found myself in a safe space to use my phone, I immediately called my neighbor Bill. My good friend Bill was a retired OB/GYN and had done well for himself most of his life. But he understood the idea that when someone is in need, we should do what is necessary to fill that particular need. Once I told Bill the situation he immediately came to assist me with enough gas in his portable gas can to get me to the gas station. Bill understood the need without ever questioning me and even offered to fill up my tank. Bill was one of the nicest men I've ever met in my life. My hope is that we all can take on the DNA of Bill and help those in need who have asked for help, and those who may never ask, because that is truest form of sowing a seed. My mother always told my brother and me as kids, "When you do right, right will come back to you."

Chapter 6

Row The Boat

One of the greatest pieces of advice I've ever received was to always find myself in life rowing the boat and never rocking the boat. In this chapter, we will explore the significant difference between the two and how to implement them actively in our lives. Rocking the boat has no purpose and direction, and rowing the boat not only has direction, but also moves the object forward.

Let's deal with rocking the boat first, and how that works against the art of appreciating others, so we can end the chapter on a high note with rowing the boat. The ideology of rowing the boat actually comes from my Boy Scout leader, Mr. Richard Collins. As a Boy Scout, I would go on camping trips and adventurous excursions that would include canoeing with my scout partners. I've always been the outdoors type of person, so my eagerness to get on the water was not in question. One of the things I quickly learned about canoeing is proper weight distribution. Weight distribution is critical to a canoe or kayak staying afloat because if it's not considered, then everyone will find themselves swimming.

How does weight distribution play a factor in the art of appreciation? No matter what side of the aisle you may find yourself on, you must equally distribute feedback and appreciation. Too much of the other could possibly have your employers, spouse, children or whatever relational type swimming with no raft to hold on to. Too much criticism without any positivity deposited will leave a tremendous void and questions such as, "Does this person actually care, or better yet, do they even like me?" On the other hand, too much appreciation without any constructive feedback will not position that person with the understanding of knowing the areas of improvement. As an individual and leader, you must find that sweet spot, like my great-grandmother used to say, "Know when to hold them and know when to fold them." It's been said over many years that too much of one thing sometimes is not the healthiest choice. Another important aspect of rocking the boat is that there is no momentum being built when the boat is being rocked. Momentum is crucial to growth. Momentum is critical to forward progression. The ultimate result from rocking the boat is horizontal movement. The overall idea for life is to grow, whether it's consciously or subconsciously. As a young child you grew daily until you looked around one day and you were 5'5," 5'7," 5'10" and so on. Vertical growth is always better than horizontal growth. Vertical growth is birthed from rowing the boat.

Before we enter the phase of rowing the boat, may I have a moment of confession? When I was a kid growing up, beyond being a Boy Scout, often my dad and I would go on one- and two-day camping trips in the woods. On these father-and-son camping trips, of course we found ourselves inside of a canoe enjoying the nice breeze and scenery, until I intentionally rocked the boat (having fun in the shallow water), and my dad would fall out into the water. I can hear his voice now that has now become our very own inside joke, "Help Len, please help me!" Why would I do such a horrible act towards my dad? There is no answer, but there is a lesson to be shared even in my mischievous ways. Whenever I rocked the boat, it cost me the price of not being able to move downstream because the very person I was trying "rock out" I then had to help "back in." There is a profound tone in that how you treat people matters and can significantly cause a domino effect on your team, church, organization or business. I've seen so many times in life that to the very people you were hurting, you will have to circle around and apologize, or you will need something from the individual that you caused emotional harm.

Now that we've discussed rocking the boat and the repercussions of the act let's chat about what is means to "Row the Boat." I literally could end this chapter with one statement: "Work with the current and not against it." The current of positivity and appreciation flows freely and naturally. What happens in life due to pessimistic attitudes, cynical hearts and toxic mindsets is that we create the narrative that is the complete opposite of our natural flow of positivity. I believe that each of us is born with the traits or characteristics of appreciation. As children between newborn and 2 years old, we expressed gratitude in some capacity without any thought. How many times have you seen a baby be fed a bottle, and when they're done, they look up and smile at the person who fed them? Total satisfaction! Amazing appreciation!

The point of that small analogy is that we were born with the DNA to row the boat and flow with the current of valuing individuals. But then we develop bad habits, sometimes intentionally and sometimes unintentionally as we travel down horrible roads. Those can be thought of as the "road of selfishness," the "all about me highway" and the "I don't care about you intersection."

Another important aspect of rowing the boat has come from an observation I made from my time in the United States Navy. Working on the flight deck of an aircraft carrier, particularly the USS Enterprise (CVN-65), required focus, determination, consistency and more importantly a team of sailors who were willing to have a row the boat mentality. It has been said that the flight deck is possibly the most dangerous job in the world. You have billion-dollar planes taking off in the middle of the ocean with speeds of 0-100 mph in 4.2 seconds. You have men and women from all walks of life working together for one common cause, and that is to serve our country in the most challenging conditions. On the flight deck everyone is color-coded according to their responsibility. Yellow shirts are the plane directors, which means basically they are the bosses of the deck. The blue shirts are some of the hardest-working individuals working to make sure the planes are secure with chocks and chains. The purple shirts are in charge of fueling airplanes and all support equipment.

The Art of Appreciation

The green shirts make sure the aircraft actually take off successfully from the flight deck. Now that you have some context as to how complex it is to work successfully on the flight deck, let's parallel that with rowing the boat.

It is unquestionable that the flight deck is dangerous, and if everyone is to remain safe and alive, EVERYONE must work together fluidly without needing anything in return but the well-being of the person standing next to you.

When you row the boat, it means that you are working together toward a common goal, and that is to get up stream. What does moving upstream mean? Moving upstream means that we're growing and allowing our lives to be transformed with each day that passes. When you are in your canoe with your partner, it is impossible to move forward if the front oar is paddling with the current, but the back oar is paddling backwards. Rowing the boat is quite easier than rocking the boat. I understand that some individuals will adopt the rock the boat mentality no matter what, but I will encourage you to work and be patient with people despite where they currently are in life. Lastly, if you want to truly live your best life, as some may call it, you must always find yourself rowing the boat because that is the only way to get upstream.

Chapter 7

Lengthen Your Runway

Have you ever gone to the airport with zero intentions of actually traveling? I have certainly done so on many occasions, with the sole intention of listening and watching the commercial airplanes take off while getting a whiff of jet fuel. Sounds like a weirdo, right? Well that is me, through and through. Since I was a little boy my love and fascination for airplanes have been deeply rooted. Not sure exactly where this fascination was birthed from, but my father was a Navy sailor, so that could be it. As I navigated through life my fascination with airplanes quickly changed to appreciation.

Appreciating the determination, grit and passion of the Wright brothers and how they changed the landscape of how we travel in the 21st century. Truthfully, the Wright brothers had no idea the impact they were going to make on modern technology and the travel industry, but they were willing to expand their minds toward reaching their goal of flying in the air. The Wright brothers ultimately forecasted the world's need before anyone could ever picture even the mere thought of flying. The primary reason the Wright brothers are considered the aviation pioneers through inventing, building, and flying the world's first successful airplane is because they were willing to expand their minds towards something greater than themselves.

The Art of Appreciation

The goal of this chapter is for every reader to understand how important it is to know the significance of expanding your mindset and lengthening your mental runway toward maximizing every moment to express appreciation, extend gratitude and personify value placement towards people in the most authentic way. Consider this question. Were you aware that a host of airplanes cannot land at various airports? As a young kid, I couldn't understand for the life of me why certain classes of aircrafts couldn't land at selected airports. The true reason for that is because of the size of the plane, the wingspan and the speed of the aircraft. There are different classes of airports, and pilots, whether it's a commercial pilot or a private pilot seeking to enjoy his recreational hobby of flying, know which airports are cleared for them to land. Can you believe it that our lives are similar to pilots, aircrafts and airport runways? Sure enough, we should mirror the runways that allow airplanes to successfully land in the sense that expanding our thoughts and perspectives can ultimately begin to paint a different picture for us in the way we express gratitude towards others.

Boeing 737 aircraft cannot land at small local airports that possibly a Cessna 152 would be able to use. The landing strip that we decide to land on will determine how we view life. Are you landing on the negativity runway or are you landing on the positive runway full of opportunity, promise and joy? It was once said, "The cheapest way to enjoy ourselves in life is to be nice to others." Those words could not be truer because we must always be mindful of how we treat others. Thus, the art of appreciation is hugely important.

Lengthening our runway is unquestionably about expanding our mindset, but let us explore another angle. The first thought and goal is being accepting of others even when they don't look like you or speak the same language. Some of my closest friends are those who don't look like me, whether that is middle class, lower class or upper class. The same individuals may not share the same political beliefs as I do, but we are able to mix and mingle and be the best of friends. Why is that? We value the person first and foremost. We value the gifts each other may have to offer, and more importantly we value the potential that we all collectively have. Our pure intention is to help each other become the greatest individuals we were created to be. I remember when I was working in the corporate sector, and we would attend trainings or possibly a conference, and I would find myself observing the movements of all attendees. Some would call that "people watching." I observed that most attendees would sit with someone they either know from the same company or someone that they have a particular connection with. I totally get why people would do that because it's familiar and comfortable. On the other hand, I would intentionally find a table full of strangers and would make introductions and proceed with healthy dialogue. Why is that? I never want to pigeonhole myself to interact only with individuals that I share something in common with. Expanding your mindset will sometimes require you to have dinner with a Muslim and yet you are a Christian. Broadening your perspective will require you to have a cup of coffee with the homeless. Gaining insight will even have you in convalescent homes volunteering your time.

In every neighborhood I've lived in, my goal was to introduce and familiarize myself of course with the layout of the community, but more importantly with my neighbors. I'm not so old school that I would bring over a "welcome to the neighborhood" pie, but I at least wanted to know who I was sharing this particular geographical location with. Once I made it over the hurdle of introductions, I soon found out various unique and interesting facts about each individual that would enlighten my mind, expand my perspective and enlarge my passion for people.

We must find the heart and spirit to narrow the gap between building relationships and staying within the comforts of our own runways. Working to close that gap will demonstrate the heart to lift others in their pursuit of becoming better individuals, which will eventually become the greatest unwrapped gift. Valuing others enough to step outside of our comfort zones is something we all can and should aspire to embrace. The concept of lengthening your runway or painting a canvas of appreciation is not about the big things—it is about the consistent things. Focusing on appreciation and placing a significant amount of attention on valuing human life in this book create an implicit indication that those things should be emulated. However, I wrote this book to show you how to better live out appreciation in your life. What I have found is that often we check the box of what we have done in the past, and there is a consequence of "checking the boxes," or using what we've done in the past, to determine our identity. Don't get me wrong; what you've done in the past is important and can certainly be the cornerstone of your DNA, but we begin to devalue the appreciation we demonstrate daily. I've learned over several years that the things that make us feel good are the things that we find ourselves driven to do on a daily basis. When people around us demonstrate a level of greatness in whatever capacity and we fail to publicly recognize those moments in the spirit of appreciation, we're making it less likely those actions will be repeated.

When we fail to recognize those moments that surround us countless times during the course of our days, we effectively erase any type of culture and any form of happiness or joy from our organizations, our communities and our lives. I would even go to the extent of saying that most moments that would even warrant a simple "Thank you" or "Good job" go unnoticed or uncelebrated. Those include the moments that you've done something great and it appeared to hit blind eyes. Placing value on the lives of others is a daily practice. Simple, impactful, appreciative behaviors can provide us with daily evidence that every soul, every heartbeat and every life matters.

www.ingramcontent.com/pod-product-compliance
Lightning Source LLC
Chambersburg PA
CBHW071201090426
42736CB00012B/2409